Successful Habits of Extraordinary People

Develop Over 7 High Performance and Effective Habits - Blueprint to Powerful Stacking Habits that Stick and Mini Habits to Achieve Any Goal

Stephen Patterson

© Copyright 2019 - All rights reserved.

The content contained within this book may not be reproduced, duplicated or transmitted without direct written permission from the author or the publisher.

Under no circumstances will any blame or legal responsibility be held against the publisher, or author, for any damages, reparation, or monetary loss due to the information contained within this book. Either directly or indirectly.

Legal Notice:
This book is copyright protected. This book is only for personal use. You cannot amend, distribute, sell, use, quote or paraphrase any part, or the content within this book, without the consent of the author or publisher.

Disclaimer Notice:

Please note the information contained within this document is for educational and entertainment purposes only. All effort has been executed to present accurate, up to date, and reliable, complete information. No warranties of any kind are declared or implied. Readers acknowledge that the author is not engaging in the rendering of legal, financial, medical or professional advice. The content within this book has been derived from various sources. Please consult a licensed professional before attempting any techniques outlined in this book.

By reading this document, the reader agrees that under no circumstances is the author responsible for any losses, direct or indirect, which are incurred as a result of the use of information contained within this document, including, but not limited to, — errors, omissions, or inaccuracies.

Contents

Introduction _____ 1

Chapter 1:
Developing Effective Habits _____ 3

Chapter 2:
Which Habits to Stick To _____ 15

Chapter 3:
The Accumulation of Habits _____ 29

Chapter 4:
Keystone Habits and Taking Action _____ 43

Chapter 5:
The Secret Habits of the Successful _____ 57

Chapter 6:
Keys to Financial Success _____ 69

Chapter 7:
Keys to Social Success _____ 83

Chapter 8:
The Effect of Genes on Habit Formation _____ 91

Chapter 9:
Stacking Habits _____ 101

Conclusion _____ 111

SUCCESSFUL HABITS
of
EXTRAORDINARY PEOPLE

DEVELOP OVER 7 HIGH PERFORMANCE AND EFFECTIVE ATOMIC HABITS – BLUEPRINT TO POWERFUL STACKING HABITS THAT STICK AND MINI HABITS TO ACHIEVE ANY GOAL

STEPHEN PATTERSON

Introduction

It may come as a surprise to learn that there are very few traits that separate the average person from the utmost successful people. In this book, we are going to discuss many topics that include: developing effective habits, which habits to stick to, the accumulation of habits, keystone habits and taking action, the secret habits of the successful, keys to financial success, keys to social success, and stacking habits. Most importantly, cover the characteristics of the successful and how they maintain their success. These are surprisingly simple and straightforward habits that virtually anyone can apply to their everyday. Whether you want to be a world-famous astrophysicist or improve your finical situation to finally losing weight and staying slim for years to come. The key to tackling any goal is having the habits to develop a mindset to do so.

As you can tell by now, there will be much emphasis placed on the formulation and maintenance of habits. This is because it is ultimately our habits that make us what we are, and if these habits are not healthy and productive ones, then we cannot expect to be healthy and productive people. The role that habits have to play in our everyday lives is not to be understated under any circumstances. If you want success in any given way, then the habits that you form are going to be the most critical factors in obtaining successes or achieving your goals.

We also discuss the keys to financial and social success within this book. When most people think of success, they tend to picture wealth and luxury. While this is not the concept of true financial success, we are still going to delve into what is. Social success is what most people are really after in life, even though people tend to focus more of their energy into achieving financial success. This is why we are also going to delve into some of the secrets of gaining social success to be more highly regarded among your peers, and your self-esteem will be bolstered.

Chapter 1:
Developing Effective Habits

It is always amazing the role that micro-habits have to play in the fostering of long-term success. People tend to wait around for magic beans when it comes to success rather than putting any hard and, more importantly, extended work into whatever it is that they are doing. They let their judgments cloud their thinking with delusions surrounding their success. It is the multitude of small steps and habits that lead to success more so than large gestures and the bets made on chance happenings. The issue that most usually face is that they put all their faith in the latter and none in the former—this leads them to make little to no progress though, as it is always the small things that accumulate to give you your successes in life.

You can look at your future like it is something that you have no control over and like it is something decided by fate that does not stop to consider any of your efforts, or you can look at your future like it is something that you can take measures to control. Thinking of it through the lens of some predetermined fate is rational because there are ultimately a lot of happenings and situations that are inevitably going to be out of your control. This is a realistic and true proposition to put forth and to accept it is part of being a grounded person. You can, however, also look at your future through the lens of a time that is more adaptable and more flexible based on what you want to do with it. This mindset is more what we would call a growth mindset, as it allows for more personal growth than does the other. Thinking of your future this way will give you much more power over your fate. If you believe that you are just being tossed about randomly by the world, then you have a much higher probability of just being tossed about randomly by it. Successful people, on the other hand, take the initiative in what they do and are usually rewarded with more control over what happens to them. To use a platitude that is thrown around very often these days, they go out and happen to things rather than sitting around letting things happen to them.

Again, the role that little habits that have to accumulate over time have to play here is never to be understated. One way to better gauge your production of these habits is to do so quantitatively. For example, let's say you make a 1% improvement on a skill every day for a year—that is a dramatic 365% improvement that you have then made by the year's end. How did you come to that? It is by small and incremental improvements that built themselves upon one another over time. It would be more or less impossible to have made that drastic of an improvement had it not been for you practicing the skill every day or, in other words, developing habits that enabled you to make such improvements.

The central concept that makes small, everyday habits so important is the concept of compounding interest. The choices that you make from day to day may not have very noticeable effects within a more limited timespan, but their results tend to accumulate over time. In other words, they "compound," causing more substantial effects—either positive or negative.

This can, however, be a bit of a double-edged sword because bad habits that develop can also have a way accumulating in their adverse effects. For example, if you go to a gas station every day and buy a can of Coke, you are going to be more likely to have a health complication at the end of the year than you would if you had bought a tea every day. Again, the effects of your everyday decisions here compound over time to lead to even more significant consequences. If you make good choices, you will see good results—if you make bad decisions, you will see adverse effects.

We tend to be more outcome-focused than we are process-focused. This is especially true in today's world, where everything that we could ever want is already given to us on a silver platter by technology. This causes us to overlook the means by which things are produced and procured. Looking for outcomes without first learning the methods by which these outcomes are created is an excellent example of wanting to know without wanting to learn—or expecting your reward without putting any work into what you are doing. These are attitudes that are all too common in today's world, but those who avoid falling for these traps see many gains for doing so.

Two of the most important hallmarks of compounding interest are the plateau of latent potential and phase transition. The plateau of unrealized potential is the period in which you are making improvements and forming new habits, but are still not seeing any results for doing so. This is a period which naturally frustrates many people because it is hard to see any effects of one's own efforts throughout this time. This plateau is, however, punctuated by another period which goes by the name of phase transition. In the phase transition, you start to see some reward for all of your efforts. When graphed this period looks like the beginning of the curve of a hockey stick. This is your delayed reward for the effort that has accumulated, and once this phase transition is met, you can then expect good things to happen in your efforts in the future. There is a brief apprenticeship period for your growth in what you do, but once this bottleneck is squeezed through you will come out of the other end with new skills at hand and new possibilities for further improvement.

Before you can reach this phase transition, however, you must first establish skills in mapping out what habits you are going to pick up. When you first start developing new habits, your progress may prove to be so slow that you feel like you are not making progress at all, or even making negative progress. This is because any rewards that you are going to reap from your newly established habits are going to be delayed and are not going to seem very important at first. It is only after sticking to these habits for a more extended period that you will see any results.

One of the most natural and most effective ways of developing new habits is by adjusting your environment according to what habits you want to build and what habits you want to get rid of. This is done most effectively by increasing the number of steps it takes for you to indulge and bad habits while at the same time decreasing the number of steps that it takes for you to develop good habits. Let's take TV for example. This is a destructive habit, so you would want to increase the amount of effort it takes for you to watch TV on a whim. This could be done by taking the batteries out of your remote and only putting them back in when you want to watch TV, which would add some seconds to the process of starting to watch your programs. You could also leave the TV unplugged until you know the name of the show that you want to watch. This would prevent you from watching TV absentmindedly with no real aim at what you are watching in particular. This would be an example of increasing the number of steps involved in indulging in a habit that is bad for you. An example of decreasing the number of steps it requires to develop a habit that is good for you would be keeping a book on your bed stand. This makes the book more readily accessible to you than would leaving it on your bookshelf.

To be human is to err, so you cannot get discouraged when you do not make the marks that you set for yourself. You are going to make mistakes in whatever you do, so all that you should ever try to control is the number of errors that you make. You can do this by going back and analyzing what lead up to your mistake, and then applying the lesson that you have learned to your further efforts in the future. The important thing here is to keep moving on in your efforts no matter what happens. If you do not stay on top of your progress, then your mistakes are bound to multiply and increase in frequency.

Successful Habits of Extraordinary People

The next point that we should touch on is the learning curve. Once you master a skill, your fluency in that skill reaches a position on the top of a bell curve and usually stays there unless you neglect to keep developing your craft. There is, however, also something called a forgetting curve, which predicts the lessening of skill and the forgetting of its components. This can be caused by not staying on top of your practicing and positive habit forming. Once this starts to occur, it is easy to lose a lot if not all of the skills that you have developed through your new habits. Once a new talent is developed it requires constant fostering and improvement to retain.

After new habits have been developed, new routines and rituals start to emerge. You can think of habits as the microcosms in these systems and methods and rituals as the microcosms here. Your habits become the building blocks for your larger routines. If you create and develop more efficient habits, then you are bound to produce more efficient methods eventually.

To build entire routines and rituals out of your habits, you must first master the art of doing what you do every day. This can often take more effort than learning the habit in of itself can, but once you get into the habit of practicing doing what you want to do every day, you will start to see lots of improvements in your performance. All too often, people get to focus more on the outcome of their goals more so than they do the means by which their goals need to be met. Getting exposed to what you do each and every day is the only reliable way to get a grasp on what you need to do to achieve your long-term goals. If you are not in the regular habit of practicing whatever it is that you need to practice every day, then you cannot expect to learn what it is that you need to do to produce what you want to.

One truism that always applies to you no matter who you are or what situation you find yourself in is that no matter your current life situation, your existing systems of habits cause these directly. The things that you do and how you act are the only good indicators of how your life is going to go. If you want to match an ideal that is different from where you are at currently, which you always will, you then have followed the steps laid out for doing so. Start by analyzing whomever it is that you look up to and then follow in their footsteps. An all too common mistake that most moderns make is neglecting to accept the fact that they have things to learn from other people. You can ultimately listen to what a person has to say in one of two ways: as you know more/better than they do or like you have something to learn from them. Listening to others in a second way will always get you further than will the first way.

Successful Habits of Extraordinary People

Ralph Waldo Emerson once said that "A man is what he thinks about all day long." You embody the things that you want to be every time you focus on doing those things. If you spend an hour everyday writing, you are playing the part of the writer in your own life for an hour out of every day. If you keep on top on your laundry and your dishes every day, you are embodying a tidier and clean person. The same is true for bad habits though. If you smoke a pack of cigarettes a day, you are representing a smoker throughout that time. If you watch TV for an hour a day, then you are embodying a TV viewer throughout that time. You can never expect to become good at something if you never spend any time representing a doer of that particular something. When you start to perform the tasks of those whom you want to be more like, then you will begin to cast votes towards your being more like those people and developing your own skill sets. In the end, you reap what you sow, and you will always wind up being worth about what you put into your skull. If you fill yourself up with junk, you are going to get the junk out. If you fill yourself up with gold, you are more likely to get gold out.

The hard thing to grasp for many people when it comes to goal setting is the fact that meeting the end goal that you have in mind is never really the critical part. What is more important is your evolution throughout the process. This is another reason why establishing productive habits is so important. It allows you to gain tools for meeting any goals so that the original purpose that you have in mind will be just one of many to come. As cliché as this may sound, it is always more about the journey than the outcome. For example, if you want to get rich would you instead do so by winning the lottery or by spending countless hours doing work that you love? Most people would choose to win the lottery, which is where most people are wrong. Let's say you win the lottery and wind up with the same skill set that you have right now. Your life is not going to be better than the version of yourself that earned that amount of money through hard work and developed too many skills to even measure along the way. The path to happiness is virtue, not pleasure. Likewise, the road to success is hard work, not blind luck.

Another essential aspect of habit performing is identity building. It is much easier to stick to the habits of something or someone that you identify with. If you identify as a pianist, for example, you are going to feel much more inclined to practice the piano regularly and developing the skill is going to feel a lot more natural to you. Once you establish a firm identity as to what you want to be, you start to build confidence in your abilities, and you then begin to develop skill more effectively.

When it comes to behavioral change, one of the most important things that you can do regarding outcomes is to make your results seem as satisfying as possible. Research suggests that behaviors that provide immediate reward tend to be performed very often, while actions that provide delayed rewards tend to be avoided. This is very unfortunate because often behaviors that offer immediate rewards wind up not producing very many great things in the long run. So, as you can see, most people avoid decisions that will benefit them in the long term. This can work to your advantage if you keep in mind to take advantage of the things that are more likely to give you better long-term rewards. If you get into these habits and avoid the habits, which only provide you with short-term rewards, then you will start to see more results further on down the line than you would otherwise.

You can better assure that you are developing habits that will give you more long-term rewards by supplementing these habits with short-term rewards. For instance, if you want to get in better shape, you could give yourself a pass to eat an ice cream cone whenever you go to the gym. This will trick your mind through classical conditioning into believing that you are getting an immediate reward for doing something that will only give you a long-term reward.

Another, and usually more effective, way of rewarding yourself in the short term for decisions that will benefit you, in the long run, is what is known as identity reaffirmation. This is the practice of reminding yourself that you are the type of person who is more inclined to do x, y, and z. Every time that you read a chapter of a book, for example, you can then take a moment to remind yourself that you are the type of person who reads a lot and that you are brilliant. This can be a better method of rewarding yourself in the short term than external rewards can be because it offers a more profound reward, that of heightened self-esteem. If you are reaffirming the identities that you want to take on in the actions that you perform, then you will be more likely to stick to your own goals and habits in the future.

Again, so much of success depends on the little habits that you have. The only way to change your life effectively is to take incremental steps towards your goals by adjusting the habits that you have accordingly. Taking these steps will beset you on all sides with all sorts of issues, but they will also help you succeed in whatever it is that you want to do in your future.

Chapter 2:
Which Habits to Stick To

When we delve into all of the habits of the most successful people among us, we invariably start to see some common themes among them all. In this chapter, we will discuss some of the most common habits of the most successful people in our culture and which ones will bolster your chances of success in whatever it is that you do. We will also take a look at some of the most detrimental habits people develop and why you should avoid some of these.

To start with, the most successful people among us read almost regularly. You cannot expect to learn anything about whatever topic it is that you want to improve on without reading up on the subject. It is also true that overlearning will lead you to much better results, in this case. Hence, the more that you read on a topic, the better you will become with regards to it. This is just common sense, but so few people read up on whatever it is that they are interested in.

All in all, Americans read a mean average of 12 books a year, which is more than some might expect. The median average, however, is only around 4. Around 88% of the most successful people in America read for at least 30 minutes every day.

We should now look into some math involving these reading statistics. Let's say you read for 30 minutes every day for a year. Going at a rate of one page per minute (which is feasible when reading most average-sized books) would put you near a rate of 30 pages per day. Learning at this rate for this amount of time would put 10,950 pages under your belt within 12 months. The average length of a book in pages is only around 300 pages, so you would read on average 36.5 books a year reading at this pace. Now, imagine if you were to limit yourself to just one or two subjects in all these readings. You could most likely become a leading expert in at least your community on whatever these subjects are. With that, you have just given yourself the same amount of readings that most college degrees on the issue would require just by avoiding the TV trap that most people usually fall for at least 30 minutes a day. Reading is not only incredibly entertaining and informative, but it is also one of the most excellent time management techniques that you can employ.

Another thing that the successful do that most of us tend to overlook is meditation. Meditation will help clear your mind from the many stressors that plague you every day. Upon beginning to get into the habit of meditation, you may not see very many results. However, once you practice meditation techniques, you will start to see more clarity in your thinking and gain much more energy for other tasks. Meditation will also improve your memory and make your decision-making processes much faster—it even boasts many physical benefits, such as decreased blood pressure and stress levels.

As you can probably imagine, developing a new skill is usually much more complicated and multifaceted as a process than it might seem at first. No matter what you are trying to improve on, there are always many different sub-skill sets that need to be put in place to do so. This will leave you feeling overwhelmed at times, which is precisely why meditation is so essential. Meditation allows you to drop everything that you have to focus on at a moment's notice. Becoming accustomed to doing so will make you much more relaxed in regards to how many things you have on your plate. You will see more clearly what the steps are that you need to take to move forward towards your goals. Dropping all of your problems for a brief amount of time gives you a new perspective on them. It allows you to look at all of your issues analytically rather than synthetically. When you do this, you stop seeing all of your problems as being part of one big burg of questions, and you start to better hone in on just what exactly is wrong in every scenario and how to fix it.

Meditation often gets a reputation as being an egg headed activity meant for yogi masters and soccer moms, but you cannot underestimate its value in improving your cognitive functioning and overall physical health.

Another important thing that the most successful among us do is waking up early. Around 50% of the wealthiest people in America claim that they usually wake up around 3 hours before their workday starts. This gives them lots of time to complete side projects, plan out the day ahead, or workout. Waking up earlier gives you an advantage because you are getting to the "meat" of the day earlier than others are. Your peak logical reasoning throughout the day occurs during the morning hours, as does your peak libido. If you are not doing anything while these occur, then you are missing out on a lot of the productive benefits that these peaks have to offer you. Taking advantage of these higher levels of cortisol and the benefits that come along with this will help you achieve your goals much more effectively and efficiently.

Successful Habits of Extraordinary People

One of the main things that people often do wrong (usually out of necessity) when it comes to waking up in the morning is, they wake up right before they have to go to work. This makes their thinking foggy and their judgment unclear when they first start their days off. It is always better to lengthen the time between your waking up and your starting work as much as possible. Do not start working 4 hours before bedtime, but you should also avoid practically waking up at work. Your brain needs time to wake up before you get into doing your standard routine.

The successful also sleep a lot. Albert Einstein, for example, always insisted that he need at least 10 hours of sleep a night to perform at his best capacity. Around 89% of the wealthiest Americans are reported as sleeping 7 to 8 hours each night. Sleeping is not only a performance enhancer when it comes to routine work, but getting adequate amounts of sleep also has very many physiological benefits as well. Neglecting to get enough sleep can cause many adverse health complications. Memory issues are among these. Sleeping helps your brain to make connections and to process and store information that it would not otherwise save. A lack of sleep can cause a decline in all types of your memory, including both long and short term.

Another effect that sleep deprivation can have on the body is mood changes. In the short-term lack of sleep can make you short-tempered, moody, and or emotionally turbulent. In the long-term effects on mood can be even more severe, ranging from anxiety and or depressive disorders, to paranoia and even psychotic disturbances. Another cognitive impact that a lack of sleep can have on you is trouble thinking and or concentrating. The connections above that your brain makes during sleep also foster problem-solving skills, creativity, and concentration. Without adequate amounts of sleep, you cannot expect any of these skills to be up to par throughout your days.

Another effect of sleep deprivation is the increased risk of accidents. Performing tasks, while you are drowsy, makes it much more likely that you are going to run into crashes while doing so. Sleep deprivation also weakens your immune system as well. This can lead you to be more vulnerable to catching illnesses that you otherwise would not have caught. You will be more likely to get sick when you are exposed to germs. High blood pressure is another adverse consequence of sleep deprivation. Statistics show that those who sleep five hours a night or less increase their risk of developing high blood pressure dramatically.

Diabetes is another disease that you have a better chance of developing if you are sleep deprived. Lack of sleep leads you to imbalances in insulin levels which can affect your blood sugar levels and increase your risk of developing type 2 diabetes. You also tend to gain much weight when you are sleep deprived. This is because the chemical messengers that are sent from your stomach telling your brain that you are full cannot work correctly when you are sleep deprived. The result of this is that you are more likely to overindulge yourself in what you eat and you, therefore, put on extra weight.

Your sex drive is another important thing that is affected by lack of sleep. Lack of sleep can cause lots of endocrine imbalances which can have adverse effects on your sex hormones, primarily testosterone in men and estrogen in women. These imbalances can cause your sex drive and your libido to lessen. Moreover, finally, poor balance can also be caused by a lack of sleep. This can make you more prone to falling and other accidents.

As you can see, an adequate amount of sleep is not only a prerequisite for success, but it is also a prerequisite for healthy living in general.

Another behavioral trait of the hugely successful is exercise. The successful do not just go to the gym to gain muscle mass. They do so to retain their overall health. Not only will exercise help your body to perform its regular functions, but it will also help your mind to perform better. Your brain requires copious amounts of oxygen to complete all of its duties regularly. Exercise will help you get enough oxygen to your brain, which will then increase your cognitive functioning. Not only will exercise keep your IQ from dropping below what it is at, but it will also improve your memory and learning abilities. Around 76% of the wealthiest Americans report that they spend at least 30 minutes a day biking and or running. This helps their bodies and minds to continue performing their normal functions.

The most successful among are always improving their communication skills. Not only are they great and clear communicators, but they are still trying to improve on this trait with nearly everyone whom they come into contact with. This makes them ready at a moment's notice to discuss more important topics reliably and straightforwardly. Spending all of your time learning things is not likely to do you much good if you are not relaying these ideas to others. After all, what good are your ideas if all that they do is stay within your head? No one can get any value out of the things that you never say. While it is essential to know what it is that you are talking about and be careful and precise in what you say, it is ultimately more important to communicate your ideas with others so that people know what you are thinking. Working on your communication skills can be one of the quickest means of improving your overall quality of life because those around you can immediately know what you want them to know. It is amazing how quickly people will be more receptive to what you have to say if you start throwing more and more of it out there. This is especially important for shy people to keep in mind. Do not be timid in what you have to say. So long as you speak to other people with respect and confidence, everything should go relatively well.

Successful people also talk to themselves quite often. This is a great way to improve your communication skills when no one else is around. This method also allows you to get a better grasp of what you are thinking about something that you are aiming for. You can better organize your thoughts regarding a topic when you write some of your ideas down and or relay them to yourself verbally. This will make your dreams more transparent and more memorable to you, and it will also make adjusting those thoughts to be more rational and useful a lot easier. You cannot expect all of your plans to follow through if you are not introspecting on them in this way.

A big factor in the merits or demerits of your communication is your ability to build your internal dialogue effectively. Mastering your internal discussions will allow you to come into conversations regarding your plans with more confidence and more effectiveness. If you go into a business meeting just ad-libbing everything that you have to say, you cannot expect to achieve the same results that you would have had you came prepared in what you have to say.

There is yet another benefit in talking to yourself that should be touched on here. Talking to yourself about things allows you to analyze specific situations with more objectivity and more rationality than you would otherwise have. You are better able to interpret what exactly you are saying when you are saying it in a way that you can hear and not just think. This allows you to put greater checks on yourself to keep yourself from just running away wildly with whatever ideas that pop into your head.

The next method that the successful use is closely related to the last one, they journal each day. When successful people do this, however, they do not just vent or aimlessly write down whatever is on their mind. Instead, they focus on their future goals and plans to achieve those goals. This is a much more reliable method of sticking to goals than just thinking about them mentally. Once you put your ideas into writing, they crystallize into something much more concrete. You are giving yourself a real, tangible starting off point in writing down your future goals. Journaling can also be an excellent means of self-care therapy. You can focus on what your problems are that you need to solve as well as what your goals are. This can help you better understand what bothers you the most and how to explain the most problematic motifs in your everyday life.

The most successful among us are also the least fearful among us. This is not to be confused with the avoidance of things that make us afraid in practice though. It is not that the successful need to avoid scary things, it's that nothing really scares them and, therefore, few things hold them back. So many of the barriers that we see before ourselves are placed there by fear of what we have yet to see. The only way to break these unnecessary barriers down is to face the things that we fear the most and to break free from the self-imposed shackles that we often find ourselves in. A lot of the times the fears that we are harboring are caused by past events which occurred long ago in our pasts. These fears are particularly harmful because they are often entirely divorced from our current reality and therefore do not help us with our current problems. It requires close thought tracking to determine which fears you have that are helping you and which ones are hurting you. Once you gain skills in doing this though, you will reap great rewards for doing so.

The successful are also more inclined to step away from their devices than the rest of us. This allows them to keep a clearer head than the rest of us do. Taking time away from your TV, smartphone, and or laptop will help you feel more natural and saner. You will also lessen your dependence on these things by doing so.

To be successful, you must keep yourself grounded as much as possible. It is all too easy to let moderate successes go to your head and to start slacking off because you believe that you are already ahead of everyone else. This is a wrong approach to take because, firstly, it is impossible to stay ahead of everyone and, secondly, you should never be comparing your success to that of others, you should instead always be comparing yourself to the person who you were the day before, with the aim of always being a little bit better than that person was. You have to check your pride at the door and admit that others may know more than you do at times to move forward.

Another trait of all of the most successful people among us is persistence. You can never expect to achieve any of your goals if you do not practice perseverance and self-discipline. It is, after all, only small and incremental steps that will get you to where you want to be when you are trying to achieve a particular goal. The adage "slow and steady always wins the race" holds here as anywhere. It is always smarter to try to accumulate your efforts and take steady steps towards the completion of your project than to expect to complete the entire thing within one day. You cannot write a symphony of any worth within 24 hours (unless you are Mozart), so instead, you need to get into the habit of working on what it is that you love to do each day.

Above are the most common characteristics that all successful people have. As you can already tell, these traits take time and energy to develop, but once you start to practice these traits, you will see great results in whatever it is that you enjoy doing.

Stephen Patterson

Chapter 3:
The Accumulation of Habits

As we have already gone over, the effects of small habits tend to accumulate and grow over time. Now, we should go over just how these effects can grow exponentially, why this is important, and how to maximize your benefits from this phenomenon.

We should start with some basic math. Let's say you get 1% better at performing a task each and every day for a year. This means that at the end of the year, you will be 36.5% better at performing the task. The equation for this looks like this: $0.1 \times 365 = 36.5\%$

You can, of course, adjust your workload based on just how much progress you desire to make and just how much time you have on your hands. If you wanted to get 10% better at performing a task, for example, then you would need to practice it for 232 days in a year under this model. This equates to 5 days per week, which is much less intensive than doing it every day.

Now, we should analyze why it is that some habits are more comfortable to stick to than others. This is an important step to take because it teaches us how to adjust our habits to be more practical and more comfortable to follow.

To analyze this in more depth, we will now examine a recent Princeton study titled "The Good Samaritan." A good Samaritan situation is when someone helps a stranger in need. Students at the divinity school at Princeton decided to put this situation to the test in the real world by administering the following study.

This study featured people who thought that they were about to give presentations on helping those in need. An actor was placed in the hallway towards the stage on which they were going to give their performances. This actor was set on the ground and was made to act like he was in pain and needed help. The participants, however, had been told before that they needed to hurry to get to the presentations, so none of them stopped to help the person in need on their way to give presentations on helping people in need.

The point of this study was to highlight the importance of systems vs. goals. The participants here were goal-oriented. They were there to give presentations, but they let their end-goals cloud their judgments on their ways of meeting this goal. It is never that the goals you set forth are the most essential part of the actions that you are taking—the most crucial part of what you do is always the system that you set forth for doing so.

While it is always important to begin doing whatever it is that you do with an end goal in mind to keep you grounded, on task, and involved in what you are doing—it is much more important that you are sticking to your repetitions of the functions that you are taking up. This will allow you to meet further goals in the future, not just the ones that you are taking up at the moment. Success is always more a matter of growth than of achievement.

The next thing that we should discuss is just how long it takes to meet individual goals. Habits typically take anywhere from 3 weeks to 8 months to become firmly developed. It is more of a lifestyle that you are aiming to establish when you are developing new habits, so once your new habits are developed, and you start to see results you cannot afford to just default to giving up and neglecting to further your progress. This is a conservative attitude to take, and it will invariably lead you back into the same old destructive habits that you started out with. Avoid all of this by staying on top of your development even after you have passed through your initial phase transition into more successful habits.

The power of repetition is not to be underestimated when considering the automaticity of a particular habit. Studies have shown that the more repetitions of something that you do, the more automatic that habit will become for you. At a certain point, however, the habit will become intuitive to you. While practicing beyond that point is still beneficial and even necessary, your skill at that point is already firmly established, and you will have a much easier time doing whatever it is that you have been practicing.

One method of more effective habit formation is what is known as the "three R's" of habit formation these are as follows:

Reminder: This is what initiates the habit. It is, in other words, your cue. For example, you could set the alarm on your phone which tells you to read for 30 minutes every day. This would be your reminder.

Routine: This is the actual act of practicing the habit itself. For example, if you are trying to get in shape going to the gym every day would be your routine for doing so.

Reward: This is what you get in exchange for the behavior. This can be the most effective way of ensuring that you stick to good habits. Without this step, there is not a visible short-term reward for what you are doing, so you drive to do so will most likely lessen with time. For example, you could reward yourself for reading for 30 minutes by then watching TV for an additional 30 minutes. This will keep you practicing that habit for longer than you would otherwise.

We should now take a look at some of the most reliable methods of sticking to the habits that you set forth for yourself.

The first method for doing this is to keep what you are doing simple. When you first start off employing a habit, you are going to be met with more difficulty if you follow the habit big and complicated. To avoid fatiguing yourself unnecessarily, you should take these three steps: 1. Start off with a habit that you find easy 2. Increase the amount of time and effort that you build into the habit, but by incremental steps and 3. Break the habit down into smaller, more digestible chunks as needed.

These methods all seem very simple and easy to follow in theory, but they prove to be too hard for some to support in practice. Everyone wants to write their own best-selling novel, but very few people are willing to sit down and take the time to write a couple dozen short stories first. It is always more important to stick to your routines rather than to get the results that you are aiming for.

The amount of motivation it takes to start off on developing a habit is always much, much more than it takes to sustain a habit. In fact, it really makes no motivation at all to support a habit. All that you have to do is just keep doing what you are already doing. For example, after running a mile in one direction, it is much easier to run another mile in the other direction to get back home. This is because you are already prepared to do so, and you know that you really have nothing to lose in doing so.

You can also accumulate the positive effects of your habits by setting up your environment in a way that is conducive to making positive gains. You should make it easier to do the things that are good for you and make it harder to do the things that are bad for you. This will make you much more likely to stick to good habits and avoid bad ones. Your goal here is to make making good decisions so easy that you just cannot say no to them.

These cues that we place in front of ourselves are what are known as triggers. Of triggers, there are two types: cold triggers and hot triggers. Hot triggers are things that could be acted upon in the present moment, while cold triggers cannot. For example, a crisp trigger would be a coupon to a restaurant that is going to open up a month from now, while a hot trigger would be a coupon to one that is already open.

Needless to say, it is hot triggers that most people find more appealing. If you want to motivate yourself or others to do something, it is always best to look for hot triggers to do so. Very few people enjoy having to think ahead and following long-term courses of action. Providing hot triggers makes benefits an immediate happening and therefore encourages operations to be performed more.

Of hot and cold triggers five factors go into them, the first of these is time. For example, let's say you have to meet deadlines for projects at work every week. If you have to turn in an invoice every Monday and every Thursday, then it is time which is the main factor driving these actions.

The second factor that affects triggers is location. For example, let's say you go to a gym every day where you do squats using a bar. In this example, it would be the location of the gym which would drive that habit. Another critical factor that affects triggers are the previous events that triggers have. These are events that cue you to perform a habit. For example, if you pray before every meal, then sitting down at the table would be the last event for prayer and prayer would be the previous event for eating.

The fourth factor that affects triggers is your emotional state. The mood that you find yourself intends to have a much more significant impact on your behavior than you might expect. For example, if you come into work in a frustrated mood, you will be much more likely to yell at a coworker if you find yourself getting into a disagreement with one. The fifth and final factor that affects triggers is other people. This factor is a very dynamic one because other people can have a vast variety of effects on our triggers. For example, if you associate yourself with people with anger issues, you are much more likely to develop anger issues yourself.

To find some of the possible triggers that you can then apply other more appropriate triggers too, you should make two lists: the first one being a list of things that you do throughout a day. Go from your morning routine to your midday routine and finally to your nightly routine and examine all of the things that you actively do throughout a day. The next list you should make is one of the things that happen to you throughout a day. These are things that are beyond your control and that you have no say over. Once you have these two lists, you will then have a good indication of all the things that might trigger you throughout a day.

If you do what is listed above and find that some of your reactions to things that happen are not very effective, you should try adjusting those reactions. Doing this will help you remain adaptable because your neuronal connections are already formed for dealing with these triggers, so now you just have to deal with the matter of adjusting your reactions, which is much easier than is experiencing entire new things. In doing this, you are going to tie your new behaviors to the same neural pathways, which will make these much more likely to stick in the long run.

Now that we have a better overview of habits in general, we should take a look at how to know what it is that you need to change and what it is that you do not.

The first step in determining what it is that you need to change in your life is deciding what it is that is distracting you from reaching your goals. One effect that we should go over here is known as the Zeigarnik effect. This is the tendency of people only to remember what is useful to them in the short term. Once you have no more immediate need for the information at hand, however, you then tend just to throw out all of the information that you just spent all of that time learning. This is a great strategy to use in the short term to achieve your goals, but it is not something that will benefit you in the long run.

When you do nothing but let your curiosity get the best of you and absorb whatever information you want to aimlessly you create large loops of more or less useless information that take up lots of your energy and leave about where you started off in the first place. Absorbing and memorizing all of these random pieces of information not only does not get you very far, but it also opens up large nagging gaps in your cognitive energy which divert much-needed energy which could otherwise be used to complete the tasks that you need to achieve in the present moment.

While working hard and multitasking are incredibly important aspects of success you should try to avoid working very much harder than need be, especially on tacks that do not directly benefit you at least in the short term. Doing so will burn out all of your fuel before you can get to the meat of what you really need to do. You may be able to do both your job and all of these other things effectively at first, but after a while, you are bound to wear yourself out if you are continually being split between all of these unnecessary things which you do not really need to do and which do not always help you out.

Another thing that excessive multitasking will deplete is your reserves of willpower. When you are always being divided among multiple elements, the likelihood that you are going to turn down lots of further opportunities is good. You have to keep in mind that no matter who you are there is only so much of you.

One way to deal with situations in which you have to multitask is to prioritize your concerns. To go after all of the things that you have to do each day all at once is to attack a full-fledged hydra. It will overwhelm you, and you will not make as much progress as you would have you just started by picking the situation apart piece by piece.

Your willpower tends to peak during the morning hours, there is then a dip in willpower right before lunch, followed by another spike in willpower right after lunch. One of the keys to having the most auspicious days possible is to ride these waves of willpower for all that they are worth, keeping in mind that they are fleeting and that they are something to be grateful for when they come.

The next step in our effort to better prioritize our efforts to ascertain what exactly it is that we should be prioritizing.

When prioritizing what you need to do with your time, it is the things that are good but not great that you need to avoid doing at all costs. These things should be avoided even more than the things that you do not enjoy doing because you will always lose track of how often you are doing these things. These are where we get into the nagging loops that we find ourselves in, and we usually have trouble getting ourselves out of these. It is a problem of plenty, not of poverty. If you were to make a list of your 25 top priorities, it would be numbered 6-25 that need to be avoided more so than any other things that you do. Again, to take all of these up for yourself would be to try in vain to slay a hydra. Remember, there is only so much of you.

Take growing a rose bush for example. If you want a rose bush to be healthy and to look good, you are going to have to prune some of the bulbs away. There is just no way around this. You cannot expect each and every lamp of a rosebush to look good. Likewise, you cannot plan for each and every one of your interests to be a good use of your time pursuing.

One tool that will help you tell whether or not you should spend your time on something is what is known as the Eisenhower box. In this bow, there are four quadrants. In the upper left quadrant, there are the things that are both important and urgent. In the upper right quadrant, there are the things that are unimportant and urgent. In the lower left quadrant, some things are important and not urgent. Finally, in the lower right quadrant, there are the things that are both unimportant and not urgent. The important things should be delved into first, especially the important things which are also critical. The trivial stuff comes second, though the unimportant things that are also not urgent should be deleted if at all possible.

That concludes our discussion on the accumulation of habits. If you keep looking into the habits that you have in your everyday life and finding things that are not helping you, then you are bound to form new and better habits which will help you achieve more of your goals in the future. The principles laid out within this chapter should give you a good starting off point for doing so.

Stephen Patterson

Chapter 4:
Keystone Habits and Taking Action

While all of your habits, from the most minuscule to the most important, determine your overall success and well being, there are a few habits that are more seminal to your growth than are any others. These habits are what are known as keystone habits. We should take the opportunity to touch on these habits and delve into what makes them so valuable.

Keystone habits are notable not only in the sense that they are the most important habits we develop but also in the sense that all of our other habits are connected and often dependent on them. For example, let's say that you work out every day. After working out, you will experience a series of changes that will affect the rest of your day. For instance, your focus will almost immediately improve and stay sharper for some time afterward. This will cause at least an hour of much intense focus for you, which will enable you to get more work done quicker and more reliably. The second change that you will notice is that you will eat better without even really thinking about it. Your body tells your mind to provide it with more nutrients when it is put under the extra demands the working out has to give. The third and final effect of working out that you will notice is that you will sleep better. Your mind and body will eventually become fatigued from the excess work that they have done, and you will be able to get to sleep quicker and sleep longer.

Working out is just one of many examples of keystone habits employed by the most successful among us. Others include meditation, going on daily walks, afternoon naps, etc. These and many others are continuously used by successful people to keep them running at their top capacity, and once these habits have been developed, they tend to trickle into every other facet of life. This can usually create positive self-reinforcing loops, which can build upon themselves and create a completely different experience for the person feeding the positive habit—though negative habits also have this tendency to metastasize throughout the rest of a person's life.

Hence, as you can see by now, keystone habits will have wide-ranging effects on the rest of your life, which can do a lot to help you with virtually everything else that you do throughout any given day. The next topic that we should discuss now is how to take action when it comes to employing new and better habits.

Successful Habits of Extraordinary People

The first step to taking action in regards to your new habits is called pre-commitment. Pre-commitment works on the notion that willpower can be depleted and that when our willpower is low, we tend to give up lots of our goals and habits. We also are less inclined to make choices in general when we do not have that much willpower. Whereas we usually are caught up among too many decisions to be able to make any effect, when we are depleted of willpower, we cannot make choices at all.

When you do this to a specific action or behavior, you decrease your likelihood of not following through with the activity or behavior when the chosen time allotment comes up. For example, if you decide to fill out a survey at 6 P.M. one day rather than just trying to do it at some random time, then you are going to be much more likely to stick to your plan and get the survey over with.

One of the most effective methods of ensuring that you are following through with the goals that you set forth for yourself is what is known as implementation assurance. This involves providing that you stick to a schedule of practice by first writing down the time and place that you are going to perform the action at. This will give you a solid reminder of what you need to do to progress and when to do so. People who write down when and where they are going to perform a task are, on average, around 50% more likely to stick to that task. It is much easier to stick to doing something once you have made something of a contract with yourself that you are in fact going to do that thing at x place and at y time.

Now that we have established a suitable method of starting a new behavior out by writing down when and where we are going to perform the task, we should get into how to stick to the new routine in the long run and how to continue to improve on it moving forward.

One method that is useful for establishing habits, in the long run, is what is known as the paperclip method. This method involves putting a set number of paperclips in a jar and moving them over to another jar every time you complete a task. For example, let's say you work in telemarketing and you have 120 paperclips in your jar. You could move one of these over each and every time that you make a sales call in a year, and by the end of the year, you would be a much more successful worker. This goes to show that no matter what it is that you do, there are usually one or two fundamental tasks involved in the work on which everything else is dependent. These are your keystone habits that determine the success of your entire enterprise, so practicing these and increasing the frequency at which you perform these tasks will help you more than working on other tasks.

Successful Habits of Extraordinary People

Another beneficial factor of this technique is the visual cue that it provides. You are always in sight of all that you have achieved so far as well as how far you have to go to meet your goal when using this strategy. You can see all of the paperclips clearly when doing this. This makes you more immediately aware of where you are at right now, which differs from the norm, where we cannot tell where we are precisely on a particular task.

To further explore how the environment can shape our behaviors, we will now take a look at a study carried out at Harvard to determine whether or not we can influence people's habits and behaviors without even talking to anyone. This was, of course, all done through manipulating the environment around the test subjects.

They used the cafeteria at Massachusetts General Hospital as their environment. As far as drinks were concerned, they placed water fountains around the cafeteria as well as refrigerators that had both water and soda in them. In one case they still included soda in the fridges, but they added more bottles of water than before. What they found, in this case, is that people were much more inclined to but water under these circumstances. In fact, water sales increased by 26%, and soda sales decreased by 16%.

This shows that 16% of the people who originally bought soda only did so because that was what was put in front of them. We can infer from this that a lot of the decisions that we make in everyday life are more based on what is in our immediate environment rather than what we think we want.

This study goes to show the importance of tailoring your own environment to make things that are bad for you harder to obtain so that all of your lazy, default decisions will be good ones. If, for example, your popcorn is placed on the top shelf of your cabinet where it requires a step stool to get to it, while your apples are placed at arm's reach, then you are going to be much more likely to eat apples of the two choices.

As you can see now, a person's behavior is significant—if not solely—influenced by his or her environment. With that being said, it is nearly impossible to achieve all of the things that you want to accomplish if you are stuck in a negative situation and are making no attempts to escape it.

Another key to taking action is, again, persistence. Let's say that you want to write better jokes. The only reliable way of doing this would be to get and stay in the habit of writing jokes each and every day. Get a whiteboard calendar and mark off every day that you write a joke with an X if you have to. If you keep doing it every day then you will start to get longer, and longer chains of X's going, it is then that you will begin to see improvement in the quality of your jokes.

There are, of course, going to be days in which you break these chains and neglect to work on whatever it is that you work on. This mental model that you should observe under these circumstances is "never miss twice." It is not that the most successful people never make mistakes and or neglect their responsibilities, the only difference here between the successful and the unsuccessful is the fact that the successful do not get into the habit of ignoring their responsibilities in the long term.

There is a zone of long-term growth that we should also touch on now. This zone is somewhere in between complete laziness and complete burnout and here is where you should stay if you want to be successful in the long term. Success is, as are all other things, all about balance, so you cannot expect to work yourself too hard or do not work at all and still get forward in life.

Next, we need to clarify one concept that is all too often reversed in the minds of most people—motivation stems from the action and not the other way around. In other words, inspiration does not come to the lazy.

Stephen Patterson

It is almost never the case that any of the great composers, for example, popped out of their beds in the morning with brilliant new ideas for their symphonies, string quartets, etc., as Hollywood would like to have you believe. All of their greatest works were, instead, usually brought about by long and tireless hours spent at their desks with their manuscript papers below their hands. If you want to get good ideas and to produce good things, you are going first to have to sit down and think what you want to produce out for yourself.

Again, you have to be selective about what you choose to spend your time doing. Here are some excellent questions to ask yourself before scheduling out time to focus on a specific task:

- What is the main reason that I have for completing this task?

- What am I going to feel like once I am done with it?

- Will this improve my life, and if so, how?

Asking yourself these questions and others like them will help you filter out any of the tasks that you do not need to perform. When stepping back and looking objectively at your reasons for completing a mission, you will get a better understanding of just how essential and or urgent the task at hand is. You can now refer back to the Eisenhower box mentioned in chapter three if you need to.

Once you have determined that a task is worth your time, you should then start to formulate a plan as to how you are going to about completing that task. This could be formatted something like this: Desired Goal - Positive Change - Clear Plan - Committed Action - Desired Outcome.

The desired goal here is clear. This is whatever you want to achieve. The positive change here would be where all of the microhabitat strategies laid out earlier would come into play. This is probably the single most crucial part of the whole plan as it is here that the tools that you use to meet all of your future goals are gained. The next step here is having a clear idea. This one is difficult because plans have the annoying tendency to meander with the change of circumstances that accompany them. In other words, what might seem like a definite plan one day is bound to be a bit different the next day. Ideas can be fickle, so it is essential to keep a few select desired outcomes in mind when progressing in your habits in the future. This will make your plans for meeting these goals much clearer. The next step that we have here is the step of committed action. This is where persistence starts to play a significant role. Again, the goal in this step is to start off chains of practice each and every day and never to miss more than two days in a row. Finally, we come to the last step, the desired outcome. This is, in other words, the fruits of our labor. If the desired result is never met, which it usually is, then it may be helpful to go back and reanalyze the way in which you went about achieving your goal.

We now need to consider two of the most common things that prevent people from ever reaching their goals. These two things are 1. A lack of self-discipline which prevents people from staying persistent in their goals and 2. A scarcity of self-efficacy which causes people to lack faith in themselves and their ability to achieve their goals.

The former of these two disadvantages are usually very clear to see by all. The latter, on the other hand, is often more concealed and harder to detect in people.

Of these two we should first discuss self-discipline. This is something that most of the entire world lacks. If you were to give the average person you meet on the street $80,000 per year for nothing there is an excellent chance that that person will not wind up producing anything of any value. This is because people just do not like to work, especially not if they see no immediate and direct benefit from working. With this being said it becomes clear that you need to continually remind yourself when working on something that what you are doing is going to be worthwhile. Otherwise, you have no incentive to continue working on the task.

The two main pillars of self-discipline are time management and persistence. When you allow yourself to waste time with trivialities and unnecessary things you are welcoming all sorts of destructive habits in their wake. You need to remain focused on the goal at hand when you are working, that way you will keep bad habits at bay and continue to build productive habits which will help you meet all of your future goals. If you remain focused on the one task that you are assigned with at any given moment, you will also gain more energy and perseverance in doing so because your mind will not be split up among all of these other factors that you do not need to be focusing on. This harkens back to the points made on nagging loops of arbitrary efforts brought up in previous chapters. By zooming in on one particular task, you can give the work more of your attention.

If you do not want to lead a mediocre life, which you do not if you are reading this book, then you are going to have to remain aware of all of the tasks that you are presented with which do not offer you much advantage and which you would be better off not focusing on. To be successful it is not just necessary to know what you want, but also to understand what you do not want.

The next trait that we should spend some time discussing is self-efficacy. Self-efficacy is the strength of belief that you have in your own abilities. When you have low self-efficacy, you tend to underestimate your own ability to meet your goals, which often makes you less likely to even start out on new projects. This makes you far less productive than you would otherwise be and it prevents you from ever moving forward in life.

Having low self-efficacy has a wide variety of effects on your entire life. Low self-efficacy often makes people hesitant to try out new things due to fear of failure, which then leads to people not leading their lives as fully as they would otherwise. If you have low self-efficacy just remember before producing anything that your only job is to put whatever it is that you make out there. Believe in what you do and put your products out there, then all you can do is let the world decide what it likes best.

People who have high self-efficacy, on the other hand, tend to approach more demanding tasks with more confidence. This often leads them into more and better opportunities and more fulfilling lives overall. People with low self-efficacy are more likely to avoid challenges and to give up on meeting or never try to meet their goals. They also more often than not believe more than any sort of change is not possible or too hard to achieve. If you want to rid yourself of self-doubt and raise your levels of self-efficacy, as well as meet any goals that you have in mind, you should try to follow the steps mentioned below:

- Identify a reason for meeting the goal

- Determine that the desired outcome is, in fact, a positive change

- Develop your self-discipline every day

- Manage your time effectively and prioritize what it is that you work on

- Recognize that your limiting beliefs are slowing you down and work on adjusting them

- Stay persistent

- Reward yourself for keeping on track in whatever it is that you do

- Repeat

So, to conclude, keystone habits are the habits which determine so much of what your life consists of surrounding these habits. To take action and to start pursuing your goals requires the adjustment of your environment, persistence in whatever it is that you do, and pre-commitment to your habits, whatever they might be, among other things. Following these procedures in going about your daily work will help you organize your production and make progress faster and more effectively.

Chapter 5:
The Secret Habits of the Successful

When most people think of success, they think of lots of money and luxury items and having a high-paying job. This is, however, a grossly misguided concept of what being successful is. While everyone has their own personal version of what constitutes success, most versions have a few things in common—among these are job satisfaction and access to the same opportunities that everyone else has. This might sound like a platitude, but it is true nonetheless: it is far more important than your heart and soul are involved in what you do than it is that you make lots of money from. If you only get money out of what you do, then that is all that you are going to be left with. Conversely, if you just get satisfaction out of an activity, then that is all that you are going to receive.

The main things that are holding us back in most of the endeavors that we take up are usually not the things that we expect. Instead, it is often our own misperceptions about ourselves that discourage us from moving forward by any larger degrees. This goes back to the facts pointed out on the topic of low self-efficacy in the last chapter; frequently, we hold ourselves back from trying new things due to self-imposed borders that we create. This, in turn, leads us to live less involved lives than we sometimes deserve.

As you have already heard, our realities are only what we perceive them to be. With this said, it would then follow that if you recognize your truth to be a bad and unwelcoming one than you are less likely to move on to better realities. You can move forward and continue to grow and change while still being satisfied with what you have at the present moment. If you make your own personal reality out to be a hellish landscape, then it will most likely become that way. Here, as anywhere, the power of positivity takes precedence over that of cynicism or even "realism." While it is important to stay grounded, all too many modern attitudes are marked by a shallow sophistication that prides itself on pessimism and cynicism.

As Hobbes once famously pointed out, civilization cannot exist without suffering. If everyone were to get whatever they wanted automatically, there would cease to be civilization itself. When you see someone who you want to emulate or something that you want to own, it is not always easy to know the pain that was required to obtain that person's status or the labor that went into producing that thing. It is this pain and this labor, however, which are the only things that make these things worthwhile. If there is never anything put into achieving something, then there will never be anything to be gotten out of it—it has no worth if no worth has been put into it.

It is this pain that is poured into the fruits of your labor that not only makes what you worthwhile but also gives you something to work to avoid. Pain can serve as a weight that you can pull against to meet your goals. Take the immigrants from third world countries who come to America and become doctors for example. These people end up accomplishing more than most born Americans because, in part, they have things to avoid in their home countries. They have seen more poverty and despair than any of the rest of us have seen, so they know that they need to work extra hard to avoid living like that again.

There are always going to be periods in your life which will shake you to your foundations. It is in these periods that all of the negative things that people tell you are going to come back to bother you to their full extent, which you need to use to your advantage here. This is why it is always so important to cut out the negative people in your life. Over the years of being around negative people, the/ negative beliefs that they will instill in you will accumulate over time and sometimes this all will boil over into you losing some of your self-efficacy. It is during these periods that your real character is going to be tested because it sometimes takes lots of strength to stick to your goals during these periods of high stress and self-doubt. Under these circumstances, you must stay persistent in whatever it is that you do and curtail self-doubt and worry as much as possible.

It is after these periods of great adversity, usually, that The Grapes of Wrath start to show themselves. It is typically true that the bigger the hits you sustain, the bigger the payoff will be for your having done so. The great gift in adversity is always the grit and the fear that it instills in us. Without any difficulty, a person becomes spoiled, lazy, and often entitled. And even after adversity, the only way to curtail some of the more self-indulgent personality traits is to continually remind yourself of some of the adverse effects of your giving up.

Here the saying runs as accurate as ever: if you upgrade your success, you enhance your problems. After we find ourselves on the other end of hard times, it is always important to remind ourselves that we are capable of getting through basically anything that is put in front of us. We should, however, still expect to be beset on all sides by adversity in whatever it is that we do and wherever it is that we go. Increasing on what it is that you do will not decrease your amount of suffering, in fact, it is ultimately only going to expand it. You may ask yourself the question under these circumstances: why is it worth it in that case? To that one answer may be that you may find that there are things that offset the cost of suffering along the path to your success. It is only by realizing this that you can turn the hardest periods in your life into the best and most productive ones. If you are using your own suffering as that source of your inspiration, then you are going to find yourself with an endless supply of inspiration, because the adversity that you face is always going to be constant.

Another very crucial factor that goes into success is confidence. We need to be continually protecting our own confidence levels throughout each and every day to make the best decisions possible and to move forward in whatever it is that we do. When you think back on all of the significant decisions that you had made recently when your confidence was low, odds are that they turned out to be less effective than the ones that you created when your confidence was high. This is because you usually make more passive, defensive, and rapport seeking decisions when your faith is low. You cannot discern your own constructive attributes, which makes you underestimate your own decision-making abilities, which in turn makes your decision making even worse. This can create an endless cycle of low confidence followed by a decrease in decision-making ability and so on and so forth.

Stephen Patterson

Now we should discuss habit formation in everyday life in greater detail. The first thing that you get to every day is obviously your morning routine, so this routine and its effectiveness can make or break the success of your entire day. One of the greatest things that you can do in the morning which is shared by all of the most successful people in the world is listing the things that you are grateful for. This will not only give you a better perspective on all of the great things that you already have, but it is also scientifically proven to be the quickest way of improving your mood at any given time. Each day when you wake up one of your first priorities should not be to get to work or finish a side project, but instead, it should be to make a brief list of all of the things that you are grateful for. Let's say that you do this for two weeks. Most of us would run out of things to list within that time period. After you have run out of things that you can list you should then look for more things that you missed the first time around. If you keep trying to fill the list with more and more things that you had not noticed initially you are bound to come up with ideas that you would never have seen otherwise. If you continue this strategy for a year you are going to end up with an entirely new perspective on life at the year's end.

Another excellent morning routine to adopt is recalling the good things that happened the previous day and thinking of what good things could happen today or what you need to get done throughout the day. These practices will both keep you grateful for the things that you have been given recently and keep you on your toes as to what you need to do next. One more great thing to do in the morning is running through some of the personal affirmation that you like best. This is a great way to change your vibrational frequency as far as attitude is concerned and to adjust whatever may some of the faultier attitudes in place within your subconscious be. Often times attitudes get placed into us so far down that we can find it hard to dislodge them. Affirmations are a great way to adjust these sometimes very pesky attitudes, especially if they are done throughout a prolonged period of time. When repeating affirmations to yourself, there are two things to keep in mind if you want to do so more effectively. One is to visualize what it is that you are saying to yourself. This will give you a mental image of what you are going for which will cement the idea into your mind much more effectively. The second thing is to formulate and maintain a clear concept of what it is that you are going for. The more you repeat our affirmations, the more real they will become. If you stick to saying just one or two things over and over again to yourself day in and day out, you are bound to see lots of results in your attitudes and how you think in your future. Some of the greatest affirmations for success are as follows: "I excel in all that I do, and success comes easily to me." "I am constantly presented with new opportunities and successes," and "I always dress for success in body, mind, and spirit." Again, if you repeat these affirmations to yourself and keep repeating them, then they will only become more and more accurate for you.

Your morning routine should then be punctuated by the quotidian tasks that you have to take upon yourself every day. After that, we move into your brunch/ midday routine. This is where most people go on meal breaks and or go to the gym. Be careful not to spend too much time on leisure throughout these hours because there is still a lot of work that you need to do for the day around this time and it is also around this time that you start to get your daily peaks in libido, energy levels, and even logical reasoning. It is throughout this part of the day that you should use any and all downtime that you may get to analyze and improve on the habits that you exhibited throughout the morning hours. This will help you set more effective goals pertaining to the rest of your day. The hours around noon are also when you are probably going to communicate with the most substantial amount of people throughout the day. It would follow that you should probably use this time to say anything that is on your mind to those around you. Just keep in mind while doing this that you still have nearly half of the day to go through so you may want to be careful about what you say as far as criticisms or confrontations are concerned.

Next, you will find yourself entering the afternoon hours. This is the homestretch of the workday, and your performance here has a direct impact on what your workload will be the next day. This only important thing to keep in mind about working throughout these hours is that you need to stay persistent in what it is that you do here. It is all too easy to let yourself get tired and start falling behind during these hours, which is a mistake that very many, if not most, people make that holds them back significantly in the long run if they keep to these annoying habits that cause this dip in productivity after lunch.

It is throughout the afternoon hours that your reaction times are at their fastest, your blood pressure peaks (which, by the way, some potassium at lunch will help curtail), and your muscle strength is at its highest. Your cortisol (a mood stabilizer) levels are also at their highest throughout the afternoon hours, which will make you think more rationally and keep you from having any drastic mood swings. It should also be noted that people are much more likely to rush what they are doing throughout these hours and therefore more mistakes are made on everyday tasks throughout these hours.

Finally, we reach the evening hours. One of your main goals on any given day is to finish all of your daily tasks before these hours so that you will be able to finish off the day with some downtime. It is during this time that we can relax and enjoy the rewards of the efforts that we made throughout the day. If you go into the evening hours with lots of work still to do, then you are not going to enjoy your time because you will have to spend it all doing things that you have to do rather than what to do.

While the evening is the best time to relax and be lazy, it would still be beneficial for you to use this time to get ahead in regards to the tasks that you have yet to do. Doing this will keep you ahead of many because not a lot of people do this with their time. All too many people out there just punch in their eight or so hours and then put little to no thought into how they are going to spend the rest of the hours in the day. Let's say you work from 9 - 5. If you go to bed around 10 each night, then you have within this schedule the time slot of 5 - 10 completely open. This is where the average person watches TV, eats, and may converse with others. If you take this time and divide hour by hour, you will start to see a lot of opportunities that you may be missing out on in regards to developing your skills and pursuing your passions with more intensity.

Successful Habits of Extraordinary People

It is typically the evening hours in which we finally get time throughout the day to do whatever it is that we want to do. The key then to using these hours to our advantage would be to define better what it is that we want to do the most. If you are just spending these hours jumping randomly from one fancy to the next, then you are bound to make no progress in anything you do. In this case, you will live like peter pan in Neverland. You will be suffocated by your own pleasures, which will not only grow old in no time at all but will also never allow you to grow in any way.

Throughout your entire day, one of the main things that you can do to be more productive is to schedule out your time. If you are not considering time than you are ignoring an entire dimension. It should be noted that you can schedule your time in any way that you like, but you are going to have to be wise about the amount of time that you devote to certain things. If, for instance, you schedule out 2 hours each third day of your life for laser tag, then you can expect to get much better at playing laser tag, but you cannot expect to learn differential calculus this way.

The secret habits of the most successful are not so esoteric as some would like for you to believe. They are, on the whole, based on common sense and are very easy and straightforward to apply to your everyday life. Remember here that success is a lifestyle. It is not just one or two choices that you make once or twice, it is the way in which you conduct yourself day in and day out. If you want to achieve long-term success in whatever it is that you do, you are going to have to make long-term adjustments in your habits and your attitudes.

Chapter 6:
Keys to Financial Success

In this chapter, we should discuss ways to manage your finances successfully. This is one area in which most people strive for success more so than in other areas. In determining how to achieve financial success, we need first to define what financial success could mean.

When we think of financial success, some of the images that come to mind can be deceiving. The word may conjure up images of luxury items and fancy foods in our minds, but financial success is more about things like security, physical comfort, free time, and peace of mind surrounding your finances. You can use the money that you earn more effectively by investing in your safety in case of any calamities you might face in the future, better food and better means of making yourself comfortable. Earning more money in less time so that you have more time to spend doing the things that you love, and having the assurance that you are prepared for anything else that might set your path in the future.

One may, and maybe the best way, to better gauge your own financial success is to keep track of the financial milestones that you come across. These could include things like paying off your first home, paying your college tuition off in full, paying off a car, and getting out of debt for good.

Before getting into tips regarding financial success, it should be mentioned that these by no means ensure that you are going to make more money in the future. These will, however, provide useful blueprints for your search on success. Some of the most excellent tips regarding finances that you may ever receive are listed below:

Make Sure to Spend Less Money Than You Earn.

This tip can be surprisingly hard to implement, especially when you find yourself in situations in which you are struggling and living paycheck to paycheck. This is especially unfortunate because this is one of the most essential tips that will be listed here regarding your financial success. When deciding what you should spend your money on, you should not underestimate the importance of differentiating between the things that you want and the things that you need. For example, a reliable vehicle may be a need for you depending on where you live, but a luxury car with all the works is always going to be a want and a wantonly. This is where all of the advertisements and sponsored content that we come into contact with on a daily basis can prove to do us a lot of harm. We are often convinced to buy things that we do not need and hardly even want without us realizing it because we are overexposed continuously to these forms of content.

Instead of buying whatever it may be that other people who do not have your best interests in mind tell you to buy on a whim, buy, at first, only the essentials that sustain yourself day in and day out. These often include things like food, toiletries, and shelter. It is only once all of these things have been accounted for that you can start spending your money on the things that you want.

Trust Your Instincts.
You cannot expect anyone else to have your own interests in mind to the same degree that you do. This is why you should always err on the side of excessive caution when it comes to making deals and or agreements with others on financial matters. You are ultimately going to be held responsible for all and any of the decisions that you make regarding your finances, so if a particular decision does not feel right to you, then you should probably avoid making it.

Fulfill the Responsibilities That You Have to Loved Ones.

Here we should discuss some essential types of insurance in case anything happens to you. You have to remember when financing that you are not the only person who is going to be affected if something wrong happens to you. The three most important types of insurance that you can purchase for the well-being of your loved ones are as follows:

Health insurance. There is an extremely high likelihood that you are going to develop some sort of medical condition or illness in your future that is going to require treatment. The costs for medical procedures, especially in the US, is very high, as you already know, so health insurance is a must despite how healthy you may be. Unless you are self-employed, one of the most effective methods of saving money on a plan is to go through your employer's system. You should also look for higher deductibles if you want to pay less for monthly premiums. Most average earning workers would be wise to look for higher deductibles than they typically do because odds are that you are not going to spend all that much on health care costs annually if you are in good health. Looking into whether or not you qualify for a health savings account (HSA) is also beneficial in your cutting down on insurance costs. This may be the most crucial form of insurance that is going to be listed here because it is usually the most immediately applicable in most people's lives.

Life insurance. If you are a young and single person then life insurance is typically going to be much more affordable because you only need to pay for your own funeral service and your casket. Older people with children, on the other hand, have to buy a plan that is going to provide their families with income beyond their deaths. These plans usually support their kids until they become adults or until they graduate from college. In the average middle-class family, the cost of raising a child to their age of 18 is around $227,000. If the child then decides to go to college, the price for doing so will be approximately $17,000 per year for tuition, room, and board. For a private four-year college, this rate is even higher at around $32,000 a year. The cost of life insurance for a young adult, however, is somewhat inexpensive. In fact, the average nonsmoker below the age of 25 can usually get a plan with payments of $25 per month for $500,000 worth of life insurance. If you are a parent with a spouse, then you should ensure that both of you have insurance plans. This will keep your children supported in case both of you die before the children reach adulthood.

Disability insurance. The odds of suffering an injury that keeps you from working for 90 days within a year are %80 for the average 25-year-old. Your own odds may be higher or lower depending on your work and your lifestyle, but on the whole, it is always beneficial to consider a disability insurance package. Do not let the fact that you are healthy right now deter you from getting this insurance. It can be astonishing just how quickly a person can go from being in good health to being disabled. Some may not realize this, but most employers offer disability insurance packages in addition to health insurance packages. Looking into these could provide you with peace of mind that you would not have otherwise.

You are always going to have responsibilities to fulfill for your loved ones, so the sooner that you start focusing on how you are going to help them out in the event of some calamity or another the better. This is especially true if you have any dependents. These people cannot afford to live without your continued support, so you are obligated to plan ahead for them in case anything terrible happens to you.

Keep and Protect an Emergency Cash Fund.
As a general rule of thumb, the amount of money that you have in your emergency fund should be equivalent to six months of your average income. For example, if you make $50,000 a year, then your emergency fund should have $25,000 in it at all times. Bad things can pop out of

the blue at any time, and often when we expect them to the least. This amount needs to be met before you consider making any long-term investments in anything else. To strategize the other way around would be to build a house on foundations of sand. While this rate of six months' income may seem needlessly high, the average time span between jobs is around seven months, so this emergency fund may not even last you the entire time period in which you are in between jobs.

One quick way to build emergency funds up offered by many employers is matching funds plans. These are company sponsored plans in which your employer will match dollar for dollar your investment, which will make it a lot easier and quicker to raise the funds you need for emergencies. Besides, these plans ensure that you will make a 100% return on your portion before making any investment earnings. For these reasons you would be wise to take advantage of any of these opportunities whenever they may come along.

Your emergency fund should always be low-risk security, so you should make sure to look into the rates offered by the US treasury bonds and notes, as well as any savings accounts provided by any banks or institutions. Credit unions are one thing, in particular, to look out for, as they will often offer higher interest rates of savings accounts that most banks will.

Make Good Use of Your Time.

You cannot rely on wishful thinking to bring you any closer to financial success. Keep in mind that the vast majority financial success is a result a lifetime accumulation, not winning the lottery or inheriting an estate. It is time and the consistent management of it that are the keys to long-term financial success.

For example, if you were to save $100 a month from age 25 to age 65 in an account with a 5% interest rate, you would wind up saving $145,000 for retirement. The important thing about saving money is that you are establishing the habit of setting aside some amount of money, no matter how small, every month.

Diversify Your Investments

Diversifying your investments is the best way to balance your risks vs. your rewards. Once you have obtained adequate insurance and adequate emergency fund, you can then start looking into making other investments. There are innumerable things that you can invest your money in, and each will have their own investment characteristics.

To start off, you may want to stick to more common stocks. These are more popular among beginners because their prices are always available and securities can usually be purchased for them with ease. Equity securities can be bought in multiple ways: as stock in a single company, as stocks in different companies within the same industry, of as stocks in various companies in different sectors. There are also some equity securities that are managed by professional managers who will most likely know more about the industry than you do. Real estate is typically more popular as a place to invest because of the income tax benefits that it offers, but real estate is also usually more expensive to buy and sell than other investments, meaning that it is harder to turn your investment into cash with real estate.

It does not matter what you decide to invest in- markets will always be volatile, meaning that prices will go up and down depending on the number of people purchasing something or another at any given point in time. We remain aware of the fluctuations in the price of stocks from day to day because they are always mentioned in news outlets, but what always flies under our radar are the fluctuations in real estate values. This is just one circumstance under which it becomes helpful to diversify your investments. No more than 10% of your investments should be placed in securities or real estate because their value is just too volatile ever to be a reliable source of income.

Take the Long Roads When Aiming for Financial Success

There is a term in investing that refers to an investor's willingness to put his or her self-up against uncertain market circumstances called "risk tolerance." A person who has high-risk tolerance is more inclined to take up riskier investments, whereas someone with low-risk understanding is more inclined to take the safer routes to wealth.

On the whole, you should avoid or get rid of investments that give you too much anxiety. If doing so does not prove to be a sound financial decision, then at least you will still gain some peace of mind having the weight of an investment that you did not know about off your chest. There are, after all, way too many great investment opportunities out there to take up any ones that you are not very sure about. The better and safer ones will allow you to meet all of your goals without losing any sleep over the decisions that you are making. If you only make the most reliable choices possible and still find that you are beset by misfortune, then do not panic, instead, find out what your best possible options are moving forward and act on them as quickly as possible. While bad investment returns cannot be redeemed, you can still move on to the next opportunity that presents itself so that you are never entirely ruined. Here again, diversifying your investments will prove to be very beneficial to you.

Get and Stay Out of Debt.

Debt can metastasize throughout all areas of your life. Once you find yourself in debt you never feel secure and taking any steps forward becomes more or less impossible. So long as you find yourself in debt, you will never be able to fully enjoy any of the things that you come across because you are always behind financially. Avoiding more debt remains essential when you are already in debt. Lots of people make the mistake of thinking that they have so much debt that there is no more in trying to curtail any future deficits. At this point, they give up hope and just continue to waste their money without any plans to manage their financial lives any wiser.

The most effective ways to avoid debt are also the most obvious: avoid excessive spending, and keep track of your payments on everything. Do not spend any money on things that you cannot afford and do not need. One way to make yourself observe this rule is to ask yourself before any purchases: do I need this or do I want this? If the answer is that you only want it, then you should not buy it if you are already in debt. It would also be wise to be wise to limit your number of credit cards because having too many will make you more inclined to spend more on everything. Keeping track of your payments is one aspect of financial success that lots of people (mostly young) have a hard time with. To do this correctly, you should write your payments down on the regular and make sure that you follow through with all of them.

If, on the other hand, you are already in debt than there are also some ways that you can get out of it quickly. The first would be only to make your payments soon so that you do not have to pay as much for APRs. The second way to get out of debt quickly would be to see if you can lower your interest rates. This can sometimes be done by asking your bank or institution to adjust your plan or by transferring your balance to a card with a lower interest rate.

Establish A Good Credit History.

Your entire financial reputation is built upon your credit score. With that being said, the merits or demerits of this score can determine your economic life. The easiest way of ensuring that this score is a good one is to make all of your payments on time. Since your credit score is an indication of your overall credit activity, you must be able to keep your credit in order in every one of these areas to maintain a good score.

It takes far more effort to raise your score than to lower it, so take extra care to ensure that you are not getting into any habits of neglecting your payments and or making any of them late. It can be hard to get out of these bad habits once they are created, and you will always be surprised at just how quickly they can ruin your score along with the rest of your financial life.

Success is not all about finances, but being comfortable and secure financially is necessary for your success in any other facets of life. Sticking to the principles laid out in this chapter will help you achieve and maintain financial success in your future. While these habits will most likely never make you rich, they will, however, allow you to live more comfortably if you apply them continuously while making your financial decisions. If you are patient and persistent in taking control of your financial life, then you will start to reap the rewards of doing so quicker than you might expect.

Stephen Patterson

Chapter 7:
Keys to Social Success

Every now and then, you come across a person who is so socially well adapted that you find yourself floored. Conversing with these people comes so naturally because of the confidence and fluency of their speech and demeanor. It can almost make you jealous at times to meet these people who have these excellent communication abilities. It is as if these people were chosen to have the world in the palm of their hands because that is precisely how having good communication abilities can feel at times. For those of us who are on the quieter end of the spectrum, it can seem almost impossible to hold oneself to these standards, but there are nevertheless some strategies that you can use to better your conversational abilities.

It is essential to keep a growth mindset rather than a fixed mindset when it comes to communication. It may seem more or less impossible to adjust your level of popularity at will, but you have to keep in mind that even if you have the worst possible reputation, nothing remains set in stone as far as your social skills are concerned. Here, we should take a look at some of the most effective ways to better your interpersonal skills and communication abilities.

Put More Effort into Showing Interest Than into Being Interesting.

There is a common misconception surrounding popularity that misleads people into thinking that the most famous people among us are the most interesting at all times. This is actually not the case. The main thing that people want to be assured of when they are speaking to others is that they are being listened to and understood by an interested counterpart. This is why it is always much more important to show a genuine interest in what others are saying when they say it. Doing this will make you much more popular than merely having the most exciting things to say.

It should also be noted that people only get bored when others are talking excessively. It does not take nearly as much to lose someone's interest than to gain it. If you drone on excessively about superfluous topics, then people will generally be less inclined to want to talk to you in the future. Giving others the room and time to speak more than yourself will always make them feel more welcomed and more socially desirable themselves. You should also make it a point to call people by their names as much as possible. Doing this will make people feel more connected to you and will project to them that you care about them.

Remain Positive When Speaking to People—But Not Overly Positive.

There is nothing more exhausting than being around an overly negative person. These people who always expect the worst out of everyone around them and are typically rather outspoken about it will suck the life out of you more quickly than nearly any other force that you will come into contact with. If you ever find yourself in a situation in which you are closer to being one of these people than not, you should make some adjustments to your attitudes and try to project that you are remaining positive. This is not to say that you have to be all sunshine and rainbows nor that you have to be otherwise inauthentic, but you should put some effort into being more positive when talking to other people.

On the whole, excessive negativity is usually much more harmful than excessive positivity, so always err on the side of remaining too positive. Doing this will make you much more desirable to others and will increase your amount of good relationships in the future. You should, however, try to find a balance in doing this to ensure that you can remain somewhat consistent in your demeanor throughout friendship.

Avoid Gossip Like the Plague That It Is.

Avoid gossip at all costs. While chatter may win you friends and or allegiances in the short term, slandering people behind their backs will always lead you toward negative consequences in the long run. Unless you want others to speak negatively about you behind your back, you should avoid doing so to others. It should also be added that gossiping about others will make those who you do so with less inclined to trust you and divulge any personal information to you because there proves to be a chance of you stabbing them in the back. Gossiping is a petty, superficial, and indirect way to communicate ideas. It does not serve you in the long run and has minimal effect in the short term.

Gossiping is also often a sign of insecurity and weakness. The entire communication strategy is based upon the premise of tearing others down to build yourself up, which is never a good way to deal with any of your problems. If you want to avoid other people sticking their noses into your business, then you should avoid doing the same to others. It is not your business whatever others' problems may be, and you are always better off focusing on how to solve your own problems first. In gossiping, you are also potentially creating victims of your own insecurities who do not deserve the treatment that they are being dealt. If you are solving your own problems, then you have no room for gossip. If you are not addressing your own problems, then you have no right to gossip. In either scenario, gossip has no place in your life.

Remain Helpful and Dependable

You should offer your assistance when and wherever you can do so with a minimum of inconvenience. We use the phrase "minimum of inconvenience" here because helping people excessively can be even more harmful than never helping anyone at all. All too often overly agreeably people spend their entire lives helping out others out of fear of abandonment among other things and get nothing in return for doing so. Instead, they are stepped all over by all those who they come into contact with and often are never able to break these chains of people who come into their lives and bulldoze over their own self-interests.

This is not to say, however, that you should never help others. Helping others will often benefit you socially. It gives you "points" concerning game theory. It should also be mentioned here the importance of following through on the promises you make. Your reputation can be damaged by unfilled promises even more so than by no promises made at all.

Serve Your Time as A Matchmaker.

It is often that people will be more drawn to you because of the people who you introduce them to. You should always make it a point to introduce people to others to make yourself more desirable by proxy. You can do this by introducing people to one another one by one, or you can form larger groups when doing things. The more gatherings that you spearhead among people you know, the more you will be perceived as that type of person who can pull people together by others.

Keeping your social network as interconnected as possible will help you forge larger bands of alliances. It will also give you a sense that you are part of something larger than yourself, almost like a community. It is here that you will start to see your number of friends increase because you have more friends in the first place. Your popularity can improve in this way exponentially. You should, however, always keep your manners in mind when out with friends though. This means that you should never neglect an opportunity to introduce a friend to others or vice versa. Ignoring to do this can make you come across as aloof or uncaring, which will make people want to avoid you in the future.

Maintain Your Self-Awareness.
You have to be able to step outside of yourself and see your personality in a more objective lens to succeed in anything in life, including making and keeping more friends. This is not to say that you should allow yourself to become overly concerned with what people think of you though. While it is essential to know how people really perceive you it is always more important to maintain some level of self-esteem. You should take

a healthy and moderate amount of stock in what others think of you just out of respect for their opinions if nothing else.

There are many things that you do on a regular basis that you might not even notice. For instance, you may wear a perpetual frown on your face that you are not aware of that other people see every day. This may alter people's' perception of you in ways that you are not even aware because you are not taking the time to look for these aspects of yourself that are flying under your own radar. Another factor in communication that people often miss is the importance of body language. The thoughts that you are thinking as well as the words that you are speaking do not always align very well with what your body is projecting. This can be problematic because often your body is communicating more about what is really going on than you are aware of. To catch essential details that your body language is indicating before others do you should always remain mindful of what you look like physically.

Eye contact is one crucial aspect of body language. Too little eye contact can give those who you talk to the impression that you are not very interested in what they are saying, while too much eye contact can make them feel intimidated or otherwise put off. The position of your arms can also communicate a lot. Crossed arms, for example, indicate standoffishness, while the direction of your arms when they are not crossed indicated where it is that you want to go or what you are interested in. You tend to point your chest and your feet at whatever it is that you are interested in, so be sure to look these at whoever you are speaking to when you talk.

The main message that you could take away from all of this is something along the lines of "to have a friend, be a friend." If you want to find success in your social life, you are going to have to put effort into relating to other people and helping them out. People are ultimately only out for themselves, for the most part, so to make your friends, you are going to need to give people whatever it is that you have to offer them. You should not, however, let yourself be taken advantage of. Give people as much as you determine they deserve from you, and you may get the same in return out of them.

Chapter 8:
The Effect of Genes on Habit Formation

All of our best and worst habits have foundations in psychological and neurobiological mechanisms. Habitual behaviors which are fixed in the brain for a certain amount of time, as well as more prospective and flexible ones, have a complex functioning and formation instead in one or multiple regions of the brain.

Of habits that are formed over a period of time, two main types should be gone over, stimulus-response (or SR) associations and more prospective and or cognitive processes. There is, however, another way of classifying these habit types that we can also use; by using the features of the neuronal activity associated with each and every habit.

Historically, habit formation has been looked at mainly through the lens of SR associations, which are usually picked up through continued habit reinforcement. These SR associations are typically made because there is simply little to no evidence indicating prospective or purposeful behavior. There is another process of learning by the name of the associated outcome (or AO). Learning these behaviors is due to a perceived reward for, usually, performing a specific task.

If, however, there happens to be a lousy reward involved in a particular task that is performed only due to specific SR associations, then a certain degree of insensitivity to the adversity associated with the task will usually be fostered. This is because the SR systems are strong enough to keep working even if the stimulus that they are after is either inadequate or ineffective. With all of this technical jargon set aside, it becomes clear here that it is easy to keep performing a task, possibly inadvertently, long after the perceived reward is still beneficial to you. This is yet another reason why any habits that are harmful to you should always be avoided in the first place; we are just not building with the mechanisms necessary to kick certain bad practices when they prove to be harmful.

SR and AO behaviors both have specific regions of the brain that they are most influenced and formed by. SR type behaviors (which function independently of perceived outcomes) are usually regulated in the following areas of the brain: the central amygdala nucleus, the infralimbic cortex, the substantia nigral compacta dopaminergic neurons, and the dorsolateral striatum. AO type behaviors (which always depend on perceived outcomes, as their name suggests) are usually caused within the associated cognitive circuits within the brain such as the dorsomedial striatum, the orbitofrontal cortex, and the prelimbic cortex.

One way to check how useful or purposeful a specific behavior happens to be is by observing the neuronal activity in the basal ganglia during the time at which the act is practiced. Throughout any sort of trial and error learning of a skill, habits are typically very much flexible and adjusted on the go. It is only later on when the habit has been sufficiently learned that it takes on a more static and solidly defined form. When you are learning how to perform a new task, it is always natural to go about whatever it is that you are doing rather slowly at first and then to work your way up towards performing the task with greater certainty and ease. There was once a study done on rats within a shaped maze which extols this happening well. When provided some type of reward for going a particular direction in the maze, the rats learned slowly and gradually to keep going in this direction and in this way, they eventually acquired whatever habit which would benefit them with the given reward. Their behaviors finally went from being sensitive to devaluation (or AO) to insensitive to it (or SR).

During these all-important periods of behavior acquisition, it is primarily the cortico-basal ganglia circuits of the brain that undergo the most significant amount of change in the activity of their neurons. Task responsive neurons often do the most firing in the periods in which tasks begin and complete. Throughout completing a particular task, these neurons are at their most inactive, especially when the work is one that is already established in the doer's brain. This gives someone performing a particular task an opportunity to relax a little and even multitask in some cases when he or she is performing an already mastered task.

Once a precise mechanism for performing a task has been created and cemented into the brain it is usually grouped together with specific other tasks of similar characteristics. This grouping together of these tasks makes neuronal connections quicker and more efficient among tasks of similar natures.

As far as the role of genes is concerned when analyzing the formation of new habits as well as the functioning of habits already established, their implications can be widely varied and not always certain. While individual genes can have profound influences on habits, there still remains lots of other factors that can have equally seminal effects on them, including psychosocial influences, external environment influences, and much, much more.

Successful Habits of Extraordinary People

The most essential components of our anatomy, from the lens of a molecular genetic standpoint, are genes, molecules, information, DNA, and proteins, among other things. The role of proteins is to hold cells together, as well as form new hormones and neurotransmitters. Proteins are made out of amino acids, which initially have to be coded by DNA. These DNA chains have to be linked together to form new proteins within the organism.

There is a significant chain of creation that looks something like this: DNA, RNA, amino acids, proteins. It should also be noted that amino acids are hydrophobic, meaning that they stay away from water as much as possible. There are also enzymes, which are usually proteins of some sort and are responsible for catalyzing cellular reactions.

Mutations in genes would here be the main thing that would cause differences among people in habit formation. Of micro mutations there are three traditional types which go as follows: firstly, there are point mutations which entail some modification of just one letter in a genotype where the letter is only replaced by another letter. These point mutations typically do not have substantial impacts on the functioning of organisms because it is always just one letter being moved around. Then there are deletion mutations, in which one or more letters within a genotype are flatly deleted from it. These usually cause more

Stephen Patterson

detrimental effects on the organism than do point mutations. Finally, there are insertion mutations in which one or more letters are inserted into a genotype. Like deletion mutations, these insertion mutations typically have more significant impacts than point mutations on an organism. One somewhat surprising fact that should here be mentioned is that ⅔ of all modifications that ever happen do not lead to any real consequences.

95% of all DNA is noncoding, meaning that it does not have any effect on any RNA being produced. All of this DNA is then regulated by specific sequences, and it is only something called a transcription factor that can change a genotype before it has been translated into RNA or any further substance. These transcription factors are only found in the mitochondria of a cell. Since a sperm cell contains no mitochondria, there is, therefore, no mitochondrial DNA in which transcription factors can be found from the father passed on to his progeny. It is only from the mother that transcription factors can be passed down to offspring.

There are also slicing enzymes that, when mutated, create two entirely new proteins. This impact is only overshadowed by the effects of mutations in promoters and or transcription factors, which cause entire networks of new proteins within an organism. It is clear here that mutations in transcription factors have much more critical impacts on the functioning of an organism than do mutations in splicing enzymes.

Many different hormones and neurotransmitters have high impacts on the formation of habits as well as other things that should now be gone over. We will here start with some essential hormones:

Vasopressin controls social behaviors. Mutations in vasopressin receptors can cause significant changes in the social mechanisms of an organism.

Cortisol is a hormone that controls stress response. Excessive or deficient levels of cortisol can have adverse effects on your endocrine system.

Adrenaline is your body's fight or flight hormone. This tells us when to panic, which is helpful in the short term but can lead to health complications in the long run.

Serotonin can serve as your body's natural antidepressant and also causes the production of melatonin, which is your body's sleep hormone.

Dopamine is the pleasure hormone which regulates reward systems. This one is especially important in habit formation regarding classical pavlova conditioning, the basic premise of which goes something like "If I am rewarded with dopamine's, I repeat the action." Any stimulus-response habit is formed due in large part to this hormone.

Of neurotransmitters, the most important ones regarding habit formation are glucocorticoids. These control stress responses among other things, so mutations in glucocorticoid receptors will affect how an organism deals with stress.

One of the best and most reliable methods of determining what a genotype does for a particular organism is a method called cross-fostering. This method entails taking an organism at birth and putting it in a new environment with new parents. From here it would be necessary to consider both the genetic predispositions of the organism as well as the characteristics of the new environment and whatever parents are in the environment. Let's take a supposedly healthy child put into a situation with a schizophrenic stepmother for example. Since the child is in an environment with that disease entity, he or she becomes much more likely to develop schizophrenia his or herself. If the child was already born with a genetic predisposition to the disorder and was still placed in the environment with the schizophrenic, then the child's risk of developing the disorder will increase even more so. The same is valid for habit formation. If you are put into an environment in which everyone around you is messy, then you will be much more likely to become messy yourself. If we had to choose one or the other, it is probably the environment that has a more significant effect on habit formation than genes, though the two often work hand in hand. The age-old question of nature vs. nurture here boils down to one point: nurture develops on what nature allows.

The law of Brownian motion states that most molecules are subjected to random oscillations in motion which are influenced by external factors. This law applies to the heritability of traits passed on through the mitochondrial DNA of a mother to her offspring. Any chromosomes that feature one specific attribute are always going to be distributed randomly among any further divisions of the cell. This makes it more or less impossible to determine whether or not an offspring is ever going to develop a specific mutation or to determine how the DNA to RNA to the amino acid to protein transition is going to occur within the offspring.

Two of the most essential genes themselves that are responsible for changes in habit formation are NPY and MAO, both of which are responsible for anxiety reactions but mutations in the MAO gene can often cause increased degrees of aggression.

Stephen Patterson

The role of genes regarding habit formation should never be given as much credence as that roles of environment and conscious decision making are. To focus on genes and or epigenetic change regarding habit formation rather than putting new habits into practice would be to hit all of the bullseyes on all of the wrong targets.

Chapter 9:
Stacking Habits

Habits are best used as little chains of performances stacked up one after the other. To stack these up most effectively, you first need to start implementing them daily. If you want to develop good habits, then it is easiest to group larger chains of individual habits together so that they can all be performed as one routine. This will ensure consistency in whatever it is that you are doing and will make performing many individual tasks much less overwhelming. The key to pulling this off, though, is persistence in the application of these tasks. These may seem like small things to observe at first, but their long-term implications accumulate over time to much loftier dimensions.

There are some steps involved in getting a habit to stick that should not be overlooked effectively. These include but are not limited to:

- Scheduling out a time for the activity;
- Identifying a trigger; and

- Planning out the steps required in performing this action.

Once you have set aside each and every component of a stack as an individual action, you must then create reminders for yourself to go through with all of these actions. If you do not do so, then you are bound to not follow through with many of your plans. Doing this can be overwhelming at first, but once you have developed these skills and others like them, you will be better able to perform all of these individual actions as an opaque whole in the future. This will improve your productivity dramatically.

If you want success in anything that you do, you are going to need to start off small. This includes mostly just building muscle memory for performing basic tasks at first. After you have completed some of these initial stages, you can then start moving on to other more complex matters. You will improve your consistency and performance over time—and eventually, the task, whatever it may be, will become more or less automatic for you.

We are now going to go over some of the most effective methods of building habits that will be beneficial to you in all of your endeavors.

Start Out with Five-Minute Blocks.

Successful Habits of Extraordinary People

The best way to ensure that you are going to follow through with a new habit every day is to make sure that the pattern is straightforward to practice. This can be done by environmental manipulation easily.

For example, if you wanted to get better at writing you, could start off small by only writing a paragraph a day. Doing this would cause forward momentum, which would, in turn, make the task much more natural to perform day in and day out as a sustained habit. You will eventually start to write more and more with each following day after a certain point.

This mini habit formation strategy can and should be applied to the stacks of habits that you put forth for yourself. In doing this, your initial stacks will not seem very large, but they will eventually grow as your individual habits increase. You do, however, have to remember to be consistent in these initial stages to get anywhere. Once you have built up some consistency, you can then start adding more and more habits to the stacks that you create.

One thing to keep in mind when forming new habits is time management. Once you have tried a habit for the first time, you can then determine just how much time it takes to complete the task. Try sticking to short time spans, five minutes for example, at first and then gradually work your way into performing the action for longer and longer lengths of time. A five-minute block of time to start out with may not seem to you like a long-time span, but even the shortest period of time spent on a task each day will invariably accumulate to equal a large number of hours over time.

Look for Small Wins.
Try to build your routines only around small habits that do not require a lot of effort to accomplish. Doing this will create lots of emotional momentum for you moving forward. If you keep this habit small and comfortable, at least at first, then this will aid you in remembering to perform them and will make habit formation much easier.

Small wins, in this case, could be defined as actions which do not require lots of willpower and are not very hard to perform. Examples of these could be taking vitamins each day, brushing your teeth, or writing a paragraph. If you start with these tasks which require little to no effort on your part, you will have more time and energy towards working on more difficult tasks. It is like Descartes' point on differentiating duties laid out in his Discourse on the method of rightly conducting the reason and seeking for truth in the sciences, you have to first focus on more manageable tasks and then move on to the more difficult tasks. It is a natural human tendency to focus on the hardest problems that we are beset with because they require the most attention, but what many people neglect to do when problem-solving is to break problems down into their smaller components and then piece together all of the steps necessary in solving the problem. If you want to avoid being overwhelmed by difficult tasks, then you need to focus on the easier tasks first.

To do this, you should track how much time it takes to complete specific tasks and then go about performing the duties that accompany the smallest amount of time before you get to anything else in a day.

Pick A Location and A Time.
It is much easier to stick to performing a task when you have already set aside a place and time for doing so. If you want to consistently complete the stacks of tasks that you set forth for yourself, then you are going to need to anchor them to specific times, locations, or combinations of both. Here are some examples of the prompts that you could set up for yourself to hold you accountable for performing your tasks.

In the morning you could set up a routine of things that you need to get done before you start your day. You could, for example, meditate, recite affirmations, and or read to start your day off on the right path. Some great ways to prompt yourself to perform these tasks every day would be to write these downs in your calendar and to keep the book you are reading next to your bed. Performing these actions each and every morning will have a very positive impact on the remainder of the day. Your mood, as well as your performance, will improve daily as a result of being persistent in these actions.

When you get to work in the morning, you could consider preparing yourself for more demanding tasks which the day is going to throw at you rather than just jumping right into all and any tasks that you need to complete. You could then start off on performing the smaller tasks that you need to complete and eventually work your way up into the larger tasks at hand. You could prompt yourself to take these steps by forbidding yourself to check your email before a certain hour, or by writing down the series of tasks that you need to complete for the day, ordered from easiest to hardest.

Next, we come to the middle of the day. This is when most people take as long at lunch as possible, so completing a stack of tasks at this time in the day will give you quite a competitive advantage in the long run. You should, however, expect to do this with little energy though, because you have just worked for 4 or so hours. This is why the tasks that you appropriate for this time need to be easier ones so that you can manage to do them with or without a lot of energy at your disposal.

Successful Habits of Extraordinary People

After performing this stack, you should then take some time (not very much) to eat. And after you eat you should then go through any habits that will carry you through the rest of the day.

These habits could include going on a walk, meditating, or working out. One good way of motivating yourself to perform these tasks is to write them down in your calendar or to keep your walking shoes by your desk if your habit is to walk.

At the end of a workday, you should always make it a point to set yourself up for success for the following day. You can do so by performing another stack at the very end of the day. Doing this will make the next morning much easier for you, the only trick here is in reserving the energy throughout the day to perform this final set. Doing this will not only lighten the following day's workload, but it will also leave the workday on a positive note that will make you more eager to get to work the next day.

Prompts for doing this could be writing in a journal some tasks that you need to do the next day, or merely doing the tasks at hand if you find the time. Doing either one of these will increase your overall productivity in the long run.

Anchor Your Stacks to Triggers.

Triggers are, in this case, defined as motivators for performing specific tasks. These can take on all forms and are the only surefire way of reminding yourself to perform particular tasks.

Of triggers, there are two main types. These are as follows: External triggers, which are triggers put forth by things outside of you that create pavlova responses to them in your actions; and internal triggers, which are triggers that take place within your mind, such as emotions, thoughts, etc.

Anchoring your stacks of habits cannot only benefit you directly, but it can also help you indirectly since building stacks of good habits intentionally can prevent you from building stacks of negative ones unintentionally. These negative stacks can have detrimental impacts on your future, so it is important to be persistent in your observation and application of the decisive stacks.

While habit triggers can be extremely useful if you apply them correctly, they can also be harmful if misused or to meet the wrong ends. Take many of the social media sites up and running today for example. Most if not all of these sites study ways to apply triggers to get people to come back for more and more content every day. This can lead people into consuming much more social media than they really need and therefore wastes people's time.

The reason that some triggers become addictive while others never even catch on is that some offer greater rewards than others do. Without applying rewards to certain triggers, you cannot expect them to stick as much as they would otherwise.

If you use triggers consciously and to your advantage, then you will have a much easier time with establishing and maintaining positive habits rather than negative ones. Using this method will lead you to a much more successful habit formation.

When positive habits are stacked well, they become much easier to follow through with and usually a bit more efficiently performed. Grouping together all of the habits that go into executing a particular task will turn it into just another move that you have to follow through with—this will make it much easier for you to develop new skill sets and to increase your productivity.

Stephen Patterson

Conclusion

Habit formation takes a long time to master so you cannot expect to get everything right just by reading one book and calling it quits. You need to, instead, keep expanding on your skills in doing this.

You should now start to apply the concepts laid out in this book to your everyday life. Make sure to be thorough when doing so if you want to reap the most significant rewards. Once you have started to apply the concepts to your everyday habits, you will begin to see results quicker than you might imagine.

It is always amazing the role that micro-habits have to play in the fostering of long-term success. People tend to wait around for magic beans when it comes to success rather than putting any hard and, more importantly, extended work into whatever it is that they are doing. They let their own judgments cloud their thinking with delusions surrounding their success. It is the multitude of small steps and habits that lead to success more so than large gestures and the bets made on chance happenings. The issue that most usually face is that they put all their faith in the latter and none in the former—this leads them to make little to no progress, though, because it is always the small things that accumulate to give you your successes in life.

Once you have finished applying each and every concept laid out in this book, you should then move on to gathering more ideas to apply to your habit formations from other sources. Doing this will help you continue to grow and expand on your skills.

If you find this book helpful in anyway a review to support my endeavors is much appreciated.

Successful Habits of Extraordinary People

www.ingramcontent.com/pod-product-compliance
Lightning Source LLC
Chambersburg PA
CBHW060617080526
44585CB00013B/864